My United States

New Jersey

NEL YOMTOV

Children's Press®
An Imprint of Scholastic Inc.

Content Consultant
James Wolfinger, PhD, Associate Dean and Professor
College of Education, DePaul University, Chicago, Illinois

Library of Congress Cataloging-in-Publication Data
Names: Yomtov, Nelson, author.
Title: New Jersey / by Nel Yomtov.
Description: New York : Children's Press, an imprint of Scholastic Inc., [2018] | Series: A true book | Includes bibliographical
    references and index.
Identifiers: LCCN 2017001058| ISBN 9780531252611 (library binding) | ISBN 9780531232910 (pbk.)
Subjects: LCSH: New Jersey—Juvenile literature.
Classification: LCC F134.3 .Y65 2018 | DDC 974.9—dc23
LC record available at https://lccn.loc.gov/2017001058

Photographs ©: cover: Richard T. Nowitz/Getty Images; back cover ribbon: AliceLiddelle/Getty Images; back cover bottom:
DenisTangneyJr/iStockphoto; 3 bottom: Radharc Images/Alamy Images; 3 map: Jim McMahon; 4 right: Alle/Dreamstime; 4
left: Mira/Alamy Images; 5 bottom: naturekat/Thinkstock; 5 top: Xinhua/Alamy Images; 7 center bottom: Christian Goupi/age
fotostock; 7 top: Erin Cadigan/Dreamstime; 7 bottom: Sean Pavone/Dreamstime; 7 center top: Dawn J Benko/Shutterstock; 8-9:
Amy Toensing/Getty Images; 11: Julio Cortez/AP Images; 12: Margie Politzer/Getty Images; 13: Bruce Wodder/Getty Images; 14:
John Greim/Loop Images/Getty Images; 15: Nicole Reina/Dreamstime; 16-17: Aneese/Thinkstock; 19: Mel Evans/AP Images; 20:
Tigatelu/Dreamstime; 22 right: Pakmor/Shutterstock; 22 left: cbies/Shutterstock; 23 bottom right: Kerrick/Getty Images; 23
center left: naturekat/Thinkstock; 23 top left: Alle/Dreamstime; 23 bottom left: Elisabeth Pollaert Smith/Getty Images; 23 center
right: Dawna Moore/Dreamstime; 23 top right: De Agostini Picture Library/Getty Images; 24-25: Science Picture Co/Getty Images;
27: MyLoupe/Getty Images; 29: Battle of Trenton, 26 December 1776 (colour litho) (see also 332831), McBarron, H. Charles
Jr. (1902-92) (after)/Private Collection/Peter Newark American Pictures/Bridgeman Art Library; 30: Pictorial Press Ltd/Alamy
Images; 31 left: Battle of Trenton, 26 December 1776 (colour litho) (see also 332831), McBarron, H. Charles Jr. (1902-92) (after)/
Private Collection/Peter Newark American Pictures/Bridgeman Art Library; 31 right: cbies/Shutterstock; 32: Howard Kingsnorth/
Getty Images; 33: The Battle of Cowpens 1781 Daniel Morgan's, 1996 (w/c & gouache on paper), Troiani, Don (b.1949)/Private
Collection/Bridgeman Art Library; 34-35: Christian Goupi/age fotostock; 36: Al Bello/Getty Images; 37: Xinhua/Alamy Images;
38: Danielle P. Richards/MCT/Newscom; 39: KidStock Blend Images/Newscom; 40 bottom: paulista/Shutterstock; 40 back-
ground: PepitoPhotos/iStockphoto; 41: Mira/Alamy Images; 42 top left: Gutekunst, Frederick, 1831-1917Library of Congress; 42
top right: Chronicle/Alamy Images; 42 bottom right: Bob Peterson/Getty Images; 42 bottom left: Heritage Image Partnership Ltd/
Alamy Images; 42 center: Bettmann/Getty Images; 43 top left: Neil A. Armstrong/NASA; 43 top right: Axelle/Bauer-Griffin/Getty
Images; 43 center left: Kevin Mazur/Getty Images; 43 center right: Jun Sato/Getty Images; 43 bottom left: RDA/Getty Images;
43 bottom center: Martin Ellis/Dreamstime; 43 bottom right: Everett Collection/Shutterstock; 44 bottom left: Clarence Holmes
Photography/Alamy Images; 44 bottom right: Science History Images/Alamy Images; 45 top: dolah/iStockphoto; 45 center: John
Van Decker/Alamy Images; 45 bottom: Nicole Reina/Dreamstime.

Maps by Map Hero, Inc.

Front cover: Victorian buildings in Cape May
Back cover: Atlantic City skyline

Welcome to New Jersey

Find the Truth!

Everything you are about to read is true *except* for one of the sentences on this page.

Which one is **TRUE**?

T or F   New Jersey fought on the side of the South during the Civil War.

T or F   More than 1,000 kinds of animals live in New Jersey.

Find the answers in this book.

UNITED STATES

New Jersey →

Contents

Map: This Is New Jersey! **6**

1 Land and Wildlife

What is the terrain in New Jersey
like and what lives there? **9**

2 Government

What are the different parts
of New Jersey's government? **17**

THE BIG TRUTH!

Honeybee

What Represents New Jersey?

Which designs, objects,
plants, and animals
symbolize New Jersey? **22**

Freshly picked
blueberries

4

Hot-air ballons

3 History

How did New Jersey become
the state it is today? 25

4 Culture

What do the people of New Jersey
do for work and fun? 35

Famous People 42

Did You Know That 44

Resources 46

Important Words 47

Index 48

About the Author 48

Eastern goldfinch

This Is New Jersey!

CONNEC

NEW YORK

Lambert Castle

Hudson

Kittatinny Mountains

Great Valley

Delaware Water Gap

PATERSON

Passaic Falls

PASSAIC

George Washington Bridge

NEW YORK

PHILLIPSBURG

Great Swamp

NEWARK

ELIZABETH

Liberty State Park

PENNSYLVANIA

Raritan

4

Princeton University

PERTH AMBOY

Sandy Hook Lighthouse

New Jersey Turnpike

PRINCETON

1

★ TRENTON

LONG BRANCH

Hadrosaurus Sculpture

N E W

JERSEY

New Jersey Shore

Barrier Islands

CAMDEN

2

ATLANTIC OCEAN

The Pinelands

Pine Barrens

3

VINELAND

Atlantic City Boardwalk

MARYLAND

Lucy the Elephant

ATLANTIC CITY

MARGATE CITY

N
W   E
S

Delaware Bay

Cape May

Cape May

0

DELAWARE

Miles

1 Princeton University

Founded in 1746, Princeton is one of the oldest universities in America. Today, it remains one of the country's most respected schools.

2 The Pine Barrens

This 1.1 million-acre (445,154-hectare) area of forests and wetlands makes up 19 percent of New Jersey's land. It is the largest area of undeveloped land between Boston, Massachusetts, and Washington, D.C.

3 Atlantic City

This coastal city is famous for its casinos and beaches. Visitors can enjoy ocean views and amusements while walking along the Atlantic City Boardwalk.

4 George Washington Bridge

Opened in 1931, this enormous bridge crosses the Hudson River to connect New Jersey to New York City. Hundreds of thousands of cars cross the bridge every day.

New Jersey has 127 miles (204 km) of coastline on the Atlantic Ocean.

CHAPTER 1

Land and Wildlife

As the fifth-smallest state in the country, New Jersey is not a very big place. However, it makes up for its lack of size with amazing **diversity** in its people, culture, and landscapes. New Jersey is a state rich in history and natural beauty. From thick forests and deep lakes to fertile farmlands, sandy beaches, and bustling cities, it is a great state to be in!

An Elevated State

New Jersey measures about 170 miles (274 kilometers) from north to south and is about 55 miles (89 km) wide. The Hudson River and the Atlantic Ocean form the eastern border of New Jersey. To the south lies the state of Delaware. To the west is Pennsylvania. New York sits along the northeastern border. New Jersey is divided into four land regions. They are the Piedmont, the Highlands, the Appalachian Ridge and Valley region, and the Atlantic Coastal Plain.

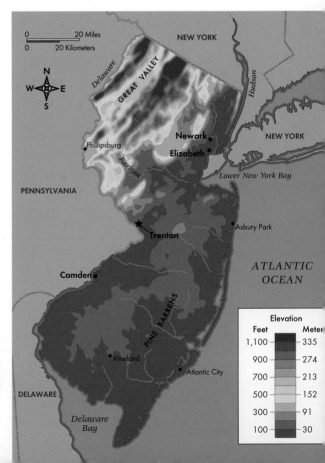

0 20 Miles
0 20 Kilometers

N
W—E
S

NEW YORK

Delaware

GREAT VALLEY

Hudson

Phillipsburg

Newark
Elizabeth

NEW YORK

Raritan

Lower New York Bay

PENNSYLVANIA

Trenton

Asbury Park

ATLANTIC
OCEAN

Camden

PINE BARRENS

Vineland

Atlantic City

DELAWARE

Delaware
Bay

Elevation
Feet | Meter
1,100 — 335
900 — 274
700 — 213
500 — 152
300 — 91
100 — 30

This map shows where higher (yellow and red) and lower (green) areas are in the state.

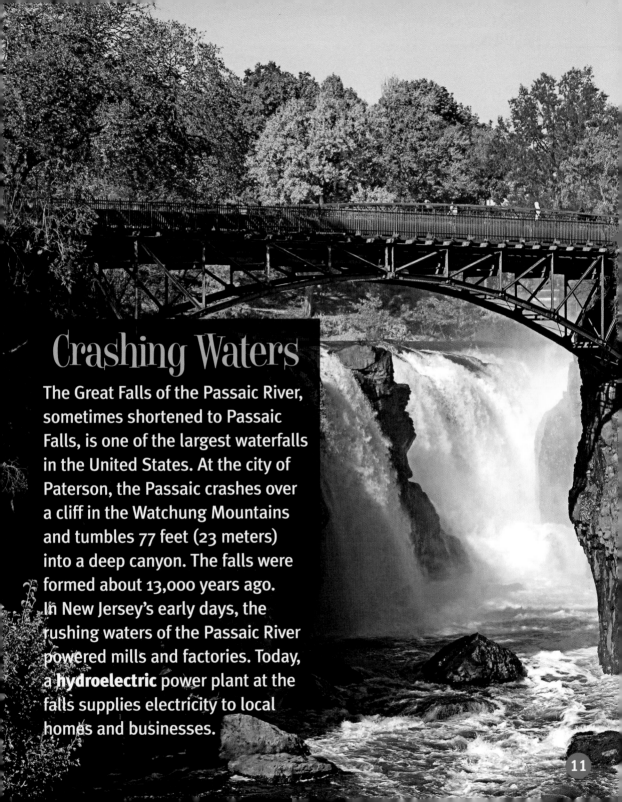

Crashing Waters

The Great Falls of the Passaic River, sometimes shortened to Passaic Falls, is one of the largest waterfalls in the United States. At the city of Paterson, the Passaic crashes over a cliff in the Watchung Mountains and tumbles 77 feet (23 meters) into a deep canyon. The falls were formed about 13,000 years ago. In New Jersey's early days, the rushing waters of the Passaic River powered mills and factories. Today, a **hydroelectric** power plant at the falls supplies electricity to local homes and businesses.

The Batsto River stretches for about 23 miles (37 km) through the Pine Barrens.

The Piedmont stretches about 20 miles (32 km) from the northeast to the southwest. New Jersey's major rivers—the Hudson, Raritan, Passaic, and Ramapo—are all located here. The Highlands lie northwest of the Piedmont. Beautiful lakes, steep hills, and valleys are in this area. The Appalachian Ridge and Valley Region lies in the extreme northwestern corner of the state. This is an area of mountain ridges separated by valleys. The Atlantic Coastal Plain, an area of rolling lowlands, covers much of southern New Jersey.

Climate

New Jersey often experiences cold winters and hot, humid summers. The state's hilly northwestern section has the coldest winter temperatures. In the south, along the coast, ocean breezes keep the area warmer during winter and cooler in the summer. Snowfall and rainfall are moderate throughout the year. **Hurricanes** and tropical storms are rare. But when they do strike, high winds and heavy downpours can cause flooding and major damage.

MAXIMUM TEMPERATURE 110°F   MINIMUM TEMPERATURE -34°F

New Jersey can get more than 2 feet (0.6 m) of snow during a big winter storm.

Water lilies are a common sight in the bogs of the Pine Barrens.

Plants

Forests cover about 40 percent of New Jersey. Hardwood trees such as maple, oak, and beech grow in the forests of northern New Jersey. Evergreens such as pines and cedars are found along the coast. These trees also grow in the Pine Barrens, a region of pine forests, marshes, and **bogs** in the south. Flowering plants such as buttercups, lilies, mountain laurels, and daisies thrive in many parts of the state. The violet, New Jersey's state flower, grows in wooded regions, fields, and lawns.

Animals

More than 1,000 different animal **species** live in New Jersey. Mammals include bears, white-tailed deer, rabbits, chipmunks, squirrels, groundhogs, foxes, and raccoons.

Almost 40 kinds of gulls can be found in New Jersey.

Cardinals, herons, geese, and seagulls soar through the skies. The Atlantic coastline is home to sea bass, swordfish, tuna, shark, crabs, clams, and oysters. Inland lakes feature sunfish and carp, while rivers **teem** with trout and catfish. About 80 species of reptiles and amphibians are found in the state.

15

The dome of New Jersey's state capitol is made up of cast iron, copper, and gold leaf.

Government

New Jersey's capitol in Trenton was built in 1792. Over the years, it has been changed, expanded, and even rebuilt after a serious fire in 1885. However, more than two centuries after it was first constructed, it remains the center of activity for New Jersey's state government. Elected leaders from all over the state gather there to make laws and carry out the government's other responsibilities.

State Government Basics

New Jersey's government is divided into three branches: executive, legislative, and judicial. The governor is the head of the executive branch, which oversees many government departments and helps lay out the state's budget. Made up of the Senate and the House of Representatives, the legislative branch of the state government makes New Jersey's laws. The judicial branch hears court cases and decides how state laws are put into effect.

NEW JERSEY'S STATE GOVERNMENT

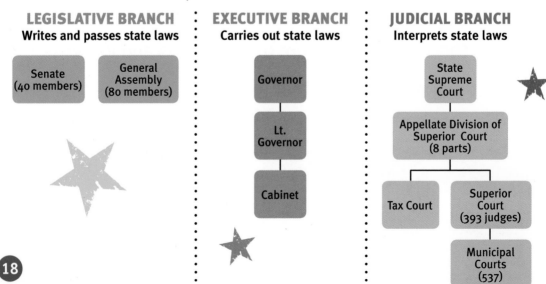

LEGISLATIVE BRANCH
Writes and passes state laws

Senate (40 members)

General Assembly (80 members)

EXECUTIVE BRANCH
Carries out state laws

Governor

Lt. Governor

Cabinet

JUDICIAL BRANCH
Interprets state laws

State Supreme Court

Appellate Division of Superior Court (8 parts)

Tax Court

Superior Court (393 judges)

Municipal Courts (537)

New Jersey's Senate has 40 members, while its House of Representatives has 80 members.

New Jersey's Constitution

The organization of New Jersey's government and laws is laid out in the state's constitution. This document also outlines the basic rights granted to the people of New Jersey, how elections are held, and more. The first version of New Jersey's constitution was written in 1776, during the Revolutionary War (1775–1783). It was revised in 1844. The state's third and current constitution was **adopted** in 1947 and amended in late 2016.

New Jersey in the National Government

Each state sends elected officials to represent it in the U.S. Congress. Like every state, New Jersey has two senators. The U.S. House of Representatives relies on a state's population to determine its numbers. New Jersey has 12 representatives in the House.

Every four years, states vote on the next U.S. president. Each state is granted a number of electoral votes based on its number of members in Congress. With two senators and 12 representatives, New Jersey has 14 electoral votes.

2 senators and 12 representatives

14 electoral votes

With 14 electoral votes, New Jersey's voice in presidential elections is above average.

Representing New Jersey

Elected officials in New Jersey represent a population with a range of interests, lifestyles, and backgrounds.

Ethnicity (2015 estimates)

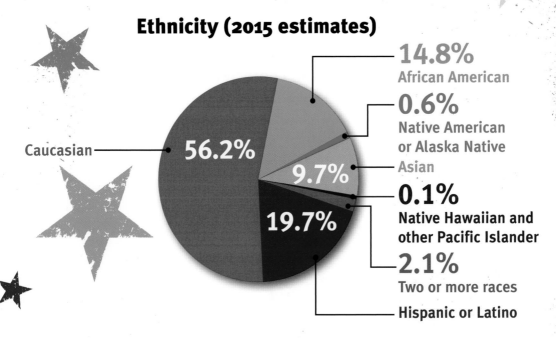

14.8% African American

0.6% Native American or Alaska Native

Asian

0.1% Native Hawaiian and other Pacific Islander

2.1% Two or more races

Hispanic or Latino

Caucasian

56.2%

9.7%

19.7%

2/3 own their own homes.

87% live in cities.

37% of the population have a degree beyond high school.

31% speak a language other than English at home.

89% of the population graduated from high school.

22% of New Jerseyans were born in other countries.

What Represents New Jersey?

States choose specific animals, plants, and objects to represent the values and characteristics of the land and its people. Find out why these symbols were chosen to represent New Jersey or discover surprising curiosities about them.

Seal

The state seal contains several symbols relating to New Jersey. The three plows on the shield represent the state's agricultural tradition. The female figures are Liberty and Ceres, the Roman goddess of grain and harvest. The helmet and horse head represent the state's independence.

Flag

New Jersey's state flag was officially adopted in 1896. Its background color is buff (a yellowish tan). The center of the flag features the seal of the state of New Jersey.

Honeybee

STATE INSECT

The honeybee was chosen to be the state's official insect in 1974 by students from the Sunnybrae School in Hamilton Township.

Hadrosaurus foulkii

STATE DINOSAUR

This dinosaur's fossils were first discovered in New Jersey in 1858.

Knobbed Whelk

STATE SHELL

This variety of sea snail shell can be found on the many beaches of New Jersey.

Eastern Goldfinch

STATE BIRD

This small bird is named for its beautiful yellow color.

Horse

STATE ANIMAL

The horse has been New Jersey's official state animal since 1977.

Red Oak

STATE TREE

This beautiful tree can grow to heights of more than 140 feet (43 m).

Scientists can learn a lot about a woolly mammoth from its tusks, including the mammoth's health, the season when it died, and how old it was.

CHAPTER 3

History

Millions of years ago, dinosaurs and other prehistoric creatures roamed the land that is now New Jersey. Scientists have discovered the **fossils** of many ancient creatures throughout the state. These include dinosaurs, 30-million-year-old sharks, woolly mammoths, and huge sea reptiles called mosasaurs. The New Jersey State Museum in Trenton has hundreds of thousands of fossils in its collection.

Native Americans

People first arrived in the New Jersey area about 10,000 years ago. These early settlers were the **descendants** of groups that crossed a land bridge that once connected Asia to North America. By about 1500 CE, people calling

This map shows the general areas where Native American groups settled.

themselves Lenapes lived in New Jersey. The Lenapes fished and hunted deer, bears, squirrels, and rabbits. They planted corn, squash, beans, and sweet potatoes, and gathered berries and nuts that grew in the wild.

Lenapes lived in small, round homes called wigwams or rectangular structures called longhouses. The frames of these buildings were built from branches placed in the ground. The Lenapes then covered the frames with sheets of bark, animal skins, and woven rush mats to provide shelter. To help fish and carry goods, Lenapes built swift canoes from tree trunks.

It was common for several families to live together in a longhouse.

Europeans Arrive

The first European to explore New Jersey was Giovanni da Verrazzano of Italy in 1524. In 1609, English explorer Henry Hudson landed in the region. Hudson was working for the Dutch, who soon built the **colony** of New Netherlands and began trading with the Lenapes. In 1664, Great Britain seized control of the Dutch land and renamed the colony New York. The Dutch land between the Hudson and Delaware Rivers was named New Jersey.

This map shows the routes of European explorers in the 1500s and 1600s.

More than 100 battles were fought on New Jersey soil during the Revolutionary War.

In time, the Lenapes were pushed off their land. Many died from diseases the Europeans had brought with them. By the 1760s, unrest had erupted between Great Britain and its colonies in North America. The colonies fought Great Britain for their independence in the Revolutionary War (1775–1783). After defeating Great Britain, the colonies created a constitution to govern their new nation, the United States of America.

Rapid Growth

On December 18, 1787, New Jersey approved the U.S. Constitution and became the third state to officially join the United States. New Jersey grew as the new nation expanded. Agriculture, industry, and transportation boomed. During the Civil War (1861–1865), more than 80,000 men from New Jersey fought on the side of the Union.

Timeline of New Jersey Events

ca. 1500 CE
The Lenape culture is established in the region.

10,000 BCE	1500 CE	1524	1609

ca. 10,000 BCE
The first humans arrive in what is now New Jersey.

1524
Italian explorer Giovanni da Verrazzano reaches New Jersey.

1609
Henry Hudson lands in the region of New Jersey and claims it for the Netherlands.

Times of War

During World War I (1914–1918) and World War II (1939–1945), New Jersey shipyards manufactured battleships. The state's many factories produced ammunition and uniforms. This meant there were plenty of jobs for the people of New Jersey. By the 1950s, the state's economy was strong. Many residents began to leave city centers such as Newark and Trenton to live in the **suburbs**.

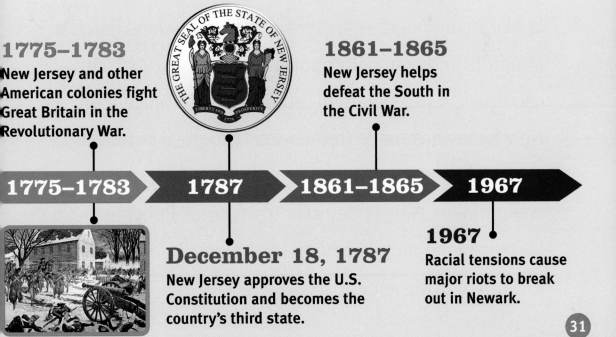

1775–1783
New Jersey and other American colonies fight Great Britain in the Revolutionary War.

1861–1865
New Jersey helps defeat the South in the Civil War.

1775–1783   **1787**   **1861–1865**   **1967**

December 18, 1787
New Jersey approves the U.S. Constitution and becomes the country's third state.

1967
Racial tensions cause major riots to break out in Newark.

As of 2015, Newark was home to 281,944 people.

New Jersey Today

As the suburbs blossomed, many cities in New Jersey fell on hard times. Businesses began to move out, and jobs became harder to find. Many neighborhoods became run-down. These problems were especially bad in black communities. In 1967, these conditions flared into riots in Newark after police officers beat a black cab driver. It took years to rebuild the city. Since then, New Jersey has made tremendous progress improving transportation, creating jobs, and cleaning up the environment. New Jersey schools such as Princeton University are ranked among the highest in the country in student achievement.

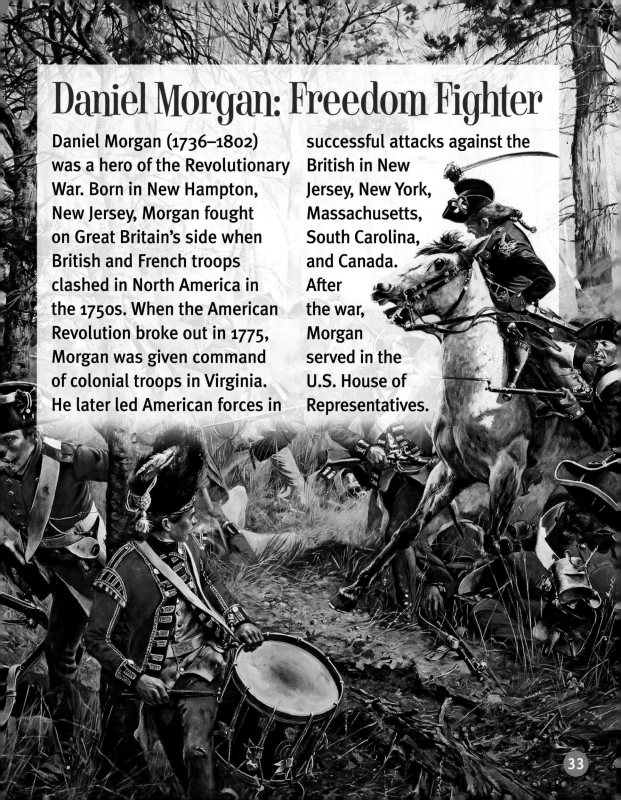

Daniel Morgan: Freedom Fighter

Daniel Morgan (1736–1802) was a hero of the Revolutionary War. Born in New Hampton, New Jersey, Morgan fought on Great Britain's side when British and French troops clashed in North America in the 1750s. When the American Revolution broke out in 1775, Morgan was given command of colonial troops in Virginia. He later led American forces in successful attacks against the British in New Jersey, New York, Massachusetts, South Carolina, and Canada. After the war, Morgan served in the U.S. House of Representatives.

More than 27 million people visit Atlantic City each year.

CHAPTER 4

Culture

New Jersey offers residents and tourists plenty of opportunities to enjoy the arts and culture of the Garden State. The state's many museums highlight local contributions to art, history, aviation, agriculture, Native American culture, and much more. Concert halls and theaters offer world-class music, drama, and dance performances.

Play Ball!

New Jersey's MetLife Stadium in East Rutherford is home to both the New York Giants and the New York Jets professional football teams. The New Jersey Devils play hockey at the Prudential Center in Newark. Major League Soccer is played at Red Bull Arena in Harrison.

For lovers of the outdoors, hilly northern New Jersey is ideal for hiking, camping, and hunting. Along the coast, swimming, surfing, and boating are popular activities.

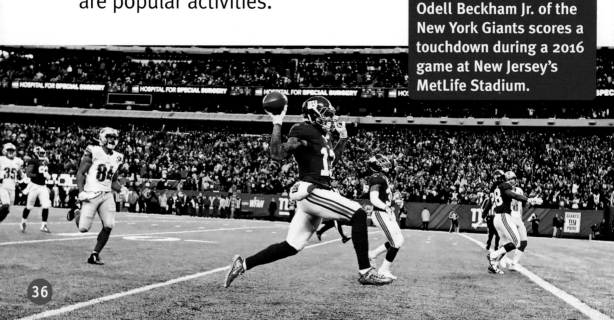

Odell Beckham Jr. of the New York Giants scores a touchdown during a 2016 game at New Jersey's MetLife Stadium.

As many as 100 hot-air balloons take off twice a day at the New Jersey Festival of Ballooning in Readington.

New Jersey Celebrations

New Jersey hosts a variety of annual celebrations and holidays. Many of them are long-standing traditions in the state. For example, every July, the town of Readington hosts a hot-air balloon festival. Other towns host annual celebrations of blueberries, cranberries, seafood, and other local specialties.

What People Do

New Jerseyans work in a wide range of businesses. Agriculture remains one of New Jersey's leading industries. Each year, farmers produce millions of pounds of fruits and vegetables. Many people work in research laboratories developing modern communications systems. Others conduct medical research and manufacture drugs and medical supplies. Hundreds of thousands of people work in the state's tourism and transportation industries.

A worker cleans equipment at a pharmaceutical manufacturing company in Kearny.

New Opportunities

The growth of important industries in New Jersey is helping to bring money into the state and providing jobs for its residents. Health care is one of New Jersey's most rapidly growing industries. Thousands of new jobs are being created in nursing homes, hospitals, and other health care services and facilities. Many New Jerseyans are also entering the financial industry. They work in banks and insurance companies, and buy and sell land or buildings.

Chowing Down

New Jersey has a reputation for its tasty blueberries, apples, peaches, cranberries, tomatoes, and corn. People also enjoy the Garden State's seafood. Steamers (steamed clams) and fried smelt are local favorites. Breakfasts often feature Jersey Taylor ham on a hard roll with egg and cheese. Saltwater taffy is a sweet treat sold in New Jersey beach towns.

 ## Italian Sub Sandwich

Ask an adult to help you!

This classic sandwich is popular throughout New Jersey. Feel free to add or remove ingredients to customize your sandwich!

Ingredients

Italian bread
Hard salami
Mozzarella or provolone cheese

Sliced tomatoes
Shredded iceberg lettuce
Olive oil
Vinegar

Directions

Slice the bread. Add one or two layers of salami and a layer of cheese. Top with plenty of tomatoes and lettuce. Add oil and vinegar to taste, and dig in!

A Great State to Be In!

The best way to appreciate the beauty and history of New Jersey is to see it in person. Stroll along the beaches and boardwalks near the shore at Cape May or Atlantic City. Visit Princeton, New Brunswick, or Trenton to learn about the state's rich history. Cheer on a local team at one of New Jersey's many arenas and stadiums. Visit a "pick your own" farm to snatch a tasty fruit or vegetable fresh off the vine. Like the tourist slogan says, "New Jersey and you—perfect together!" ★

There are more than 250 blueberry farms in New Jersey.

Famous People

Grover Cleveland

(1837–1908) was the 22nd and 24th president of the United States. He is the only New Jersey native ever to become president.

Stephen Crane

(1871–1900) was a novelist and short-story writer, best remembered for his Civil War novel *The Red Badge of Courage*. He was born in Newark.

William Carlos Williams

(1883–1963) was an American poet whose long work *Paterson* tells the story of the New Jersey city on the Great Falls of the Passaic River.

Frank Sinatra

(1915–1998) was a singer and actor whose professional career spanned more than 50 years. He was born in Hoboken.

Norman Mailer

(1923–2007) was a novelist, playwright, and journalist who won Pulitzer Prizes for his novels *The Armies of the Night* (1968) and *The Executioner's Song* (1979).

Edwin "Buzz" Aldrin

(1930–) is a former U.S. astronaut who was one of the first two humans to land on the moon and the second to walk on it. He was born in Glen Ridge.

Martha Stewart

(1941–) is a businesswoman and TV celebrity who gained worldwide fame for her skills in cooking and home remodeling. She was born in Jersey City.

Bruce Springsteen

(1949–) is a singer-songwriter and guitarist whose songs about working-class Americans have made him an international rock superstar. He was born in Long Branch.

Meryl Streep

(1949–) is a versatile movie and TV actress and singer who was born in Summit. She has won three Academy Awards and eight Golden Globe Awards.

Whitney Houston

(1963–2012) was a singer, actress, producer, and one of pop music's best-selling artists of all time. She was born in Newark.

Shaquille O'Neal

(1972–) is a former National Basketball Association (NBA) superstar who was a 15-time NBA All-Star and the winner of four NBA world championships. He was born in Newark.

Kirsten Dunst

(1982–) is known for her portrayal of Mary Jane Watson in the *Spider-Man* movies. Born in Point Pleasant, she began her career at age three as a child fashion model in TV commercials.

Did You Know That...

New Jersey is one of the smallest states, covering just 8,729 square miles (22,608 square kilometers).

Texas is 31 times bigger than NJ.

New Jersey's highest point is called High Point. It sits at 1,803 feet (550 m) above sea level.

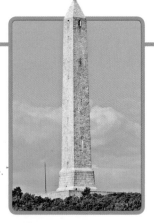

The first known organized baseball game played took place in Hoboken in 1846.

New Jersey is nicknamed the Garden State because it is home to more than 9,000 farms!

With an average of about 1,200 people living in every 1 square mile (2.6 sq km), New Jersey is the most densely populated U.S. state.

Did you find the truth?

F New Jersey fought on the side of the South during the Civil War.

T More than 1,000 kinds of animals live in New Jersey.

Resources

Books

Nonfiction

Cunningham, Kevin. *The New Jersey Colony*. New York: Children's Press, 2012.

Meinking, Mary. *What's Great About New Jersey?* Minneapolis: Lerner Publications, 2016.

Fiction

Blume, Judy. *Superfudge*. New York: Dutton, 1980.

Sheldon, Dyan. *Confessions of a Teenage Drama Queen*. Cambridge, MA: Candlewick Press, 1999.

Movies

13 Going on 30 (2004)

Paul Blart: Mall Cop (2009)

The Purple Rose of Cairo (1985)

War of the Worlds (2005)

Visit this Scholastic website for more information on New Jersey:
★ www.factsfornow.scholastic.com
Enter the keywords **New Jersey**

Important Words

adopted (uh-DAHPT-id) accepted a new way of doing things

bogs (BAHGZ) areas of wet, marshy ground where the soil is made up mostly of rotting plant material

colony (KAH-luh-nee) a territory that has been settled by people from another country and is controlled by that country

descendants (di-SEN-duhntz) your descendants are your children, their children, and so on into the future

diversity (di-VUR-suh-tee) a variety

fossils (FAH-suhlz) bones of an animal or plant from millions of years ago, preserved as rock

hurricanes (HUR-uh-kainz) violent storms with heavy rain and high winds

hydroelectric (hy-droh-uh-LEK-trik) using the power of water to produce electricity

species (SPEE-sheez) groups of similar living organisms that can breed with other members of the group

suburbs (SUHB-urbz) areas on or close to the outer edge of a city made up mostly of homes, with few businesses

teem (TEEM) to be very full of animals or people moving around

Index

Page numbers in **bold** indicate illustrations.

animals, 15, **23**, **24–25**
Appalachian Ridge and Valley region, 10, 12
Atlantic City, **7**, **34–35**, 41
Atlantic Coastal Plain, 10, 12

Batsto River, **12**
Beckham, Odell, Jr., **36**
boardwalks, **7**, **34–35**, 41

Civil War, 30, 31, 42
climate, **13**
coastline, **8–9**, 15
constitution, 19, 29, 30, 31

education, 21, 32
elections, 19, 20
elevation, 44
ethnic groups, 21
exploration, **28**, 30

famous people, **42–43**
farming, 26, 30, 38, 40, **41**, 45
festivals, **37**
flowers, 14, **23**
foods, 26, 37, **40**
forests, 7, 14
fossils, 25

George Washington Bridge, **7**
Great Britain, 28, 29, 31, 33

health care, **39**
Highland region, 10, 12
Hudson, Henry, 28, 30
Hudson River, **7**, 10, 12, 28

Italy, 28, 30

jobs, 31, 32, **38**, **39**

languages, 21
Lenape people, **26–27**, 28, 29, 30

manufacturing, 31, **38**
maps, **6–7**, **10**, **26**, **28**
Morgan, Daniel, **33**
music, **42**, **43**

national government, 20, 30, 31, 33, **42**
Native Americans, **26–27**, 28, 29, 30
New Jersey State Museum, 25
Newark, 31, **32**, 36, 42, 43

Passaic Falls, **11**
Paterson, 7, 11, 42
Piedmont region, 10, 12
Pine Barrens, **7**, **12**, 14
plants, **14**, **23**
population, 20, **32**, 45

Readington, **37**
recipe, **40**
Revolutionary War, 19, **29**, 31, 33

sports, **36**, **43**, **44**
state government, **16–17**, 18, 19
statehood, 30, 31
symbols, **22–23**

timeline, **30–31**
trees, 14, **23**, 27
Trenton, 17, 25, 31

Verrazzano, Giovanni da, 28, **30**

wetlands, 7
World War I, 31
World War II, 31
writing, **42**

About the Author

Nel Yomtov is an award-winning author who has written nonfiction books and graphic novels about American and world history, geography, science, mythology, sports, science, careers, and country studies. He is a frequent contributor to Scholastic book series.

NOV 1 6 2018